© Copyright 2015 Registration Number TXu 1-959-278

ISBN 978-1-7329254-3-4

All rights reserved. No part of this book may be reproduced or transmitted in any form or by any means, electronic or mechanical, including photocopying, recording, or by any information storage and retrieval system, without permission in writing from the copyright owner.

Any reproduction without express written consent is subject to fines and legal prosecution to the fullest extent of the law.

Author:

    Rene' Gordon

Publisher:

    ReneWritesBooks
    www.ReneWritesBooks.com
    ReneWritesBooks@gmail.com

Other books by Rene' Gordon

The Next 31 Days:
Realign Your Thinking, Realign Your Life

Life, Love, & Loss:
Words from the Heart

Animals In Our World: A – Z

...and more

DISCLAIMER

The characters depicted in this story aren't necessarily fictional or nonfictional. Any person in this story resembling a real person may or may not necessarily be that real person. It may or may not be completely coincidental that any character in this story sounds like you. Laughing out really loud.

Chapter 1: Who?

Who am I? Born in one country, raised in another.

First and middle name called by each, but not by the same.

Megan Riley. Riley at home and Megan at school.

Mama wasn't supposed to raise no fools.

So I was gonna be smart and study hard.

I was good.

I stood tall even though I was a little shorty.

I didn't get into too much trouble.

Listened to my mama...most of the time.

I guess nobody's perfect.

This is all just scratching the surface.

I'll get deep later...I promise.

I'm just putting a little perspective on it.

I was a tiny little thing, loved to dance and sing.

I was too shy though. But not at first.

Mama said I would stand on the coffee table and shout "I---!"

Then start rocking my hips from side to side.

I guess I was born to perform. It's the norm for any kid to dream.

I guess even back then I dreamed I would one day sing.

Yes, I sing...not too bad either.

Carry a pretty good tune if I do say so myself.

Not bragging, just being real.

You gotta give yourself props and acknowledge your gifts.

That's why they were given to you...

to share and bless other people with what you can do.

Anyway, my mama was a sweet lady. She was married but now a single mother.

Mother of 7 but 6 by the same. One with a different last name.

Don't make me no never-mind, still my blood.

Nothing half about it, full in every way, every day, all day.

I thought it was all good.

I was good.

I had my toys, my sisters and brothers, my mama, and my daddy.

I was happy.

I had no problems at all. Winter, spring, summer, fall,

I was happy all year long. Playing outside in the snow...

when it would snow in my little city. It was pretty.

I don't even remember being cold.

I would build a snow man...with my brothers and sisters of course.

But later on, my voice might get a little hoarse.

I would get sick...just that quick.

Out playing in the snow then next thing you know, to the doctor I go.

Penicillin, sometimes a shot in the butt cheek. That was NOT cool!

But I played, was happy, had no worries, had my family.

It was good.

I was good.

'Til the bad dreams started. The witch was chasing me.

Scrunched up face looking all ugly and twisted and frowned up hard.

Long, crooked, pointy fingers, her long, white, flowy dress trailing behind her.

She chasing me, mama chasing her, me running in circles all around in the front yard.

It was too hard.

Too hard to deal with. All that running all the time.

I guess it wasn't *good* after all.

Wake up, wake up! Make it stop!

Who is she? She looks just like my mama but a witch version.

My mama is not a witch. The witch is bad.

I wish I had not fallen asleep.

My mama is trying to save me.

She gave me life and she's protecting me from death.

The witch will kill me and take me away.

Go away!

I have to make her stop. I'm tired of running.

Who am I running from? Feels like I been running forever.

      I never, ever, NEVER, been this scared.

Except for when my dead granddaddy would come in my dreams.

He put his fist over my lips, so I couldn't scream.

He wanted to take me away.

Away with him.

Away from my mama.

Away to death.

Why is everybody trying to kill me?

Who is this man? He is **not** the granddaddy I know.

Did I really *know* him though?

I told mama 'bout the dream.

She said 'your granddaddy loved you. Never would hurt you. I can tell you that for sure.'

I didn't dream 'bout him coming for me anymore.

My mama made the bad granddaddy in my dreams go away.

But the witch kept coming.

The door would close, and I knew she was coming next.

See that's how it would start.

That's the first part.

The door closes.

I suppose that's a representation of something.

I don't know, ask Dr. Phil...shout out Doc.

Before, it was the teddy bear. He would move by himself.

Then later on, it was the doll. The doll's head would turn, without me moving her at all.

But now it's the door closing. The witch is coming.

I know it's a sign of something.

Who is she? Why is she always chasing me?

What did I do? Does she chase other children too?

This is crazy. Or maybe I'm crazy. I feel crazy sometimes.

Crazy for letting this witch chase me.

Can't she see? I'm a child from a broken home.

Leave me alone!

PLEASE God!

But God won't make her go away. My mama can't even chase her away.

It's up to me now.

"You bitch!"

"I'm tired of your ass coming in my room."

"This is MY ROOM!"

"There's no room for you here."

"I'm closing the door this time."

"The reign of your terror is over. It's done."

Stay the hell away from me and my home."

I'm punching her in her stomach, screaming at her, fussing and cussing her out.

"Get out!"

She disappears right in thin air.

I stop and stare.

I don't care.

She's gone.

I'm alone.

All alone in my room.

I didn't even wake my mama. She slept through it all.

Back to sleep I fall.

I was asleep the whole time, but it seemed so real.

What the heck is the deal?

Who was this person fussing and cussing out the witch?

I don't cuss like that.

I guess I do now.

Is that what it takes?

Acting a fool, cussing people out to get them to leave you alone?

That's wrong. Has to be wrong. I don't wanna talk like that.

But it worked.

Is this the new me? Is this who I am?

Well I'll be damn!

High school is gonna be much easier now that I found my voice.

It's my choice. I make my own rules now. Everybody can **suck it**!

High school started out cool. Loved the first two years.

Good friends, good grades, good times, no tears.

Now it's all fake. I made a mistake.

My boyfriend is the quarterback for his high school football team.

Is this real or a dream?

I'm dating the quarterback! Hot diggity darn!

Me!

The poor little girl from the broken home who gets lunch now for free.

Wow! He loves me, and I love him.

He looks like LL Cool J and I love me some LL Cool J. God knows I do!

Of course, Michael Jackson is still my first husband and my first boo.

Always will be too.

But my boyfriend is here now. Wants me to do things....mmmh

...I don't know about this now.

I mean, we kiss. That's good.

He's good. Darn good at it.

It was sweet.

Innocent.

But now he's touching everything and everywhere.

It's kind of weird. Makes me uncomfortable honestly.

But I don't stop him. He's the quarterback for goodness sake!

And he loves me, but is this a mistake?

I let him touch. I let him feel. But then he tries to, well, you know.

It doesn't happen though.

I guess I'm too scared. I'm only 16. Not ready to play on that team.

Too soon.

Too young.

He must be too young too

because he couldn't get anything anywhere it was supposed to go.

Sad, but it was kind of funny though.

He asked me not to tell his brother.

Guess he wanted his brother to think he was *the man*.

I don't understand.

He can look like *the man* while I look like *a ho*.

What's that? That's wack. No!

But again, I keep quiet and let him say what he wants to say. It doesn't matter anyway.

I know the truth.

But I should have spoken up. What would you do? Would you risk your quarterback boyfriend, star of the team, a real dream? for one little white lie? I should have called him a bitch, like I did that witch. Nah, no big deal. Let him feel like he did something special.

Whatever...

But I did finally give in a few years later. He said he loved me.

'I love you. Let me love you', his exact words.

Bull!

He just wanted to get it, hit it, then quit it, and dismiss it.

That's exactly what he did.

Pig! Trick ass pig!

He only wanted it because he found out...no...

he *thought* I had given it to somebody else before.

I did, but not who he thought. Not the way he thought.

It was my boyfriend. A different one. I initiated it this time.

It's gonna be on my terms, my way.

Not like that day...with the quarterback.

This was special.

Real.

This one really did love me.

His mama loved me too.

His whole family loved me. It was cool.

I loved them all too.

Welcomed me as family. Me!

But he got into some stuff he shouldn't have. I had to let him go.

Sad face...

I made a big mistake later. I went to a party that ended horribly.

I found myself alone with a dude. He was *not* good, and I was *stupid*.

I should have screamed.

He was fighting me, I was fighting for my life, my dignity.

I lost.

I lost more than I could ever have imagined or known.

I was ashamed to go home.

Next thing I know, I'm getting a call the next day.

It was a friend, or so I thought anyway.

He asked me, 'Did you do it? Did you really do it? And don't lie.'

Really?

Why?

Why is he asking me this? Doesn't he know me better?

We dated, or as much as 13-year-olds could.

We played tag, hide and go seek, really...not hide and go get it..hee hee.

We didn't do that.

We were innocent.

Should I tell him what really happened? Would he believe me?

I couldn't really say 'no I didn't' because I kind of did, but it wasn't like what he thought.

I was caught between a rock and a hard place.

A rock and a hard place? What the heck does that even mean?

Should I tell him I lost? Do like I did with that witch?

Tell him so he can cuss out that bitch?

It's his fault, not mine.

Tell somebody this time!

Girl tell!

TELL!

Oh well...here comes that closed door again.

The witch is coming.

"Yes" was my feeble reply.

'That's all I wanted to know.'

Click!

Dial tone...

Tears, years of friendship gone.

Tears, innocence gone.

Tears, I want to be gone.

So that's why my quarterback boyfriend did what he did.

He got wind that I said yes and admitted to something that was, but really wasn't.

So he wasn't gonna miss out on it. Not if I was giving it away like that.

He was getting it today. He was getting his way.

Pig!

Another punk ass bitch ass pig!

My quarterback? Imagine that!

Now the rumors are flying around school. I feel like a dumb fool!

Word spread from one city to another. It was all over.

I didn't do that! Well hell, I may as well.

So I go back out with the perp later.

Yeah, I was stupid. But if I'm gonna be called a ho, let's cover the tracks.

Make it look like a relationship, go out, date, yeah like that.

I'm all in. Full of sin. I'm gonna end up in hell.

Oh well! ...

    Friends turn on you, more rumors are flying too.

Fake people 'smiling in your face, all the time they wanna take your place'.

Shout out O'Jays.

I used to sing that to them in class.

Would rush out of mine to get to them fast, before they walked out.

I drew pictures of different kinds of knives..ice pick, meat cleaver, steak knife, an ax.

"Which one will it be today?", I would ask.

They acted like I hadn't just said what I did. Wouldn't even look up at me. Fake ass kids!

'The back stabbers, back stabbers'. I sang the song and even did a dance.

Too funny but really, too sad.

They saw me and heard me too. I got my point across.

But I wish I had NOT gone to that party.

I hate school.

Found a little poster of an ostrich with his head stuck in the sand.

And there I stand.

In his same place...the same space.

Gotta get out of this place.

By any means necessary.

The medicine cabinet has a few things in it. Will that do?

One of these, a couple of those, this one here too.

Only take a few. Too many and you're through.

But isn't that the point?

Here goes...

Lay down, scared, sick, sleepy.

Want to go away and never come back any other day.

Like the "Rain Rain" song, but not really. It's silly.

Too much of a chicken to take the whole bottle.

So now I'm nauseous and pissed.

Would you look at this?

Ain't this a real son of a ...oh well.

Probably not a good idea anyway.

All that chasing the witch mama did to save me would have been in vain.

A waste of time if I check out now.

No, not now. Mama would be sad.

Scrunched up witch face turned to limp arms and numb face sad.

But honestly, at that point in time, I was wishing I had.

But thank God I'm still here.

      When the shit hits the fan, you find out who your real friends are.

I had a few. I guess I always knew it was just a few.

They knew I wasn't a ho. I hope they did. They were *"the reals"*.

No matter what other people were saying, *the reals* were staying true.

Thank God for that.

Graduation couldn't come sooner. Deuces to all of you.

All of you fake ass, trick ass, phony ass suckers.

I'm getting good at this cussing thing.

Hell yeah! Kiss my ass! Ha!

That school can burn to the ground for all I care.

I don't care. Burn to ashes that drift away in the air.

Why should I care? My last two years were hell there.

Oh well, off to college now.

      A new beginning. Time for some winning.

I am a new person. Y'all don't know my past. I'm free from my past now.

Scholarship, good grades, dean's list. Just like what I used to know.

Only one problem though.

Two from the shithole school I used to go to came with me to the new.

What now will I do?

Shit!

That's ok because here comes a new boyfriend.

Aw hell...here we go again.

Same shit, different day, place, time, scene.

Didn't I learn anything?

They take what they want and don't care what I say.

I do the same darn thing.

Gotta keep seeing him now. Otherwise I *am* a ho if I let him get it and go.

What *is* this mess?

Okay, okay.

You'll be okay.

He loves you. You love him too.

Sound familiar?

Wow...not again! Dumped again. Why? And again I cry.

What did I do wrong this time?

Ok. Whatever. Next!

But this isn't too different from the last.

On to the next one... then...son of a b---,

And the next one...mother f---.

Why am I stuck on the same darn person just with a different face?

Gotta get out of this place.

And the next one...ok this is some bull!

Some bull-crapping, gosh darn, funky butt, pooing booty, screwed up CRAP!

You all know what words I really want to say, but I gotta stop all this cussing.

It's not cool.

Anyway, it's my fault though. Why don't I know better?

The common denominator is me. Has to be my fault you see.

Can't be everybody else's. It's me.

Wow!

Can't change you, so I need to change me.

Easy to say but harder to do. Oh, not for you?

Trying being me. Just try being me!

For one day. Be me one mother freaking day, trick!

My life is a living hell. I want to go away again.

I have no real friends. That's how it feels.

Do you know that feeling when you walk down the sidewalk or through the halls and all you feel are eyes staring at you with each step of your shoe heel?

That's a bum deal.

I don't want to feel anything else. So I get wine coolers and drink.

Drink the pain away.

I don't hold my liquor well so that doesn't go very well.

I walk over to his dorm.

This is the first one I mentioned...the new boyfriend.

I'm backing up a little again...my bad.

So I walk over and he's hanging up some stupid crap on his walls.

I don't remember what it was at all.

I was drunk, and it was my birthday.

Silence.

"Oh, so you don't even say anything? Hi, hello, not even happy birthday trick? Nothing?" He asks, 'Are you drunk'?

"No", I lied.

But by now, I'm playing with a pocket knife,

so he knows I'm probably drunk or at least tipsy.

I want to stab that knife right into his throat.

Kill him, bury the body outside in the courtyard.

If I was strong enough...and invisible...I would do just that.

But God wouldn't like that.

I've done so much to disappoint Him already. Can't add murder to it.

That's a top ten commandment.

You *thought* you were going to hell before?

You *certainly* would if you killed this fu-, fu-, ok...sucker.

Whew...that was close.

Just walk out the door. So I do.

What a fool.

Sigh...

Breathe...

Cry...

Chapter 2: What?

What is it about? It's all about perception.

I think I need to back it up a little.

I started to tell you 'bout the fam but skipped right to the middle.

So let me go back and give you the facts.

Now I'm told that five different people can see the same car crash,

but you will get five different stories if you ask.

Seven of us plus Mama makes eight.

If you can get even two of the same story, then that's great.

But I doubt it.

Some may be similar, and others couldn't be more far apart.

Everyone has their own perception of what is in their heart.

It's not that they are embellishing or lying, it's just their truth.

There's no denying that.

Well, this is my truth, my story, my side.

I don't have anything to hide.

Of course, I'm going to change the names...

...to protect the innocent...

...if anyone in this story really *is* innocent,

but I'll spare them the possible humiliation.

Not everyone will be able to handle the truth and handle what I'm saying.

Everything seemed okay. At least I saw it that way.

I had toys, two dogs, a cat, and at one time even a guinea pig.

The guinea pig died, but it probably could have been saved.

Shots people! Immunizations, that is.

Poor guinea pig didn't have to meet an early grave.

My brothers and sisters were pretty cool.

Everybody was school age, learning, living, playing, being a family.

I thought everyone was happy.

One sister seemed like all she did was listen to music all day.

Every album she had she would play, all day, every day.

'Get out of my room' she would say.

I never listened, and she let me stay... sometimes.

Her name is Delia. Delia was the oldest...*in the house* that is.

My mama had an older kid.

She was with my grandma.

I would get on Delia's last nerve.

I was always in her stuff...perfume, records, flute, baton...she was in the band.

She could spin that baton and flip it up with one hand,

turn around and catch it in the other again.

Whatever else she had, I would get into it.

She didn't know at first that I would do it.

But then she found it missing, used up, empty, or almost gone.

I didn't know it then, but I looked up to her.

Maybe that's why I was always in her room, in her stuff, in her space,

watching her sing and trying to keep her pace.

I wanted to be like her.

I don't think I've ever said that out loud.

I was proud to have a big sister so talented.

Did she know how good she was? I knew.

I wanted to be good like her too.

Wow!

The things you figure out when you start thinking and looking back.

Sometimes it's good to do that.

    My oldest sister in *age* was grown.

She had a family of her own.

She lived with her husband and daughter. Her name is Amelia.

That's why I said Delia was the oldest in the house, but Amelia was my oldest sister.

I didn't really know much about her when I was younger.

She was more like an aunt than a sister.

Another father but the same mother.

A sister nonetheless and you better not say otherwise.

I'll punch you dead in your eye...U-N-I-T-Y. Shout out Queen Latifah.

Anyway, I got to know her much better when I was a little older.

You see me and her daughter...her name was Sasha...played together all the time.

Singing in the back yard, songs and nursery rhymes.

It was cool.

It was good.

I was good.

My oldest sister was nice, and I never thought twice about a difference.

A sister is a sister, and love is love.

Then there was LeShae. She was like a second mama to me I would say.

She was the only one who could wash and comb my hair and I wouldn't care.

If anyone else would try, I would cry.

Not even my own mama could get away with it unless she bribed me.

So you see, my sister LeShae was it for me.

I was tender-headed, and she was the only one who knew how to handle it.

She would take her time and comb my hair gently.

She was the best!

She treated me more special than the rest.

It was like I was her daughter, not her sister.

She was my sister mama, mama sister.

I found out later there was a reason for her actions.

A reason she kept me so close.

She was protecting me from the monster.

But I'll get into that later.

    Ellis was my oldest brother.

There's not a lot about him that I remember from when I was younger.

He wasn't home a lot or something.

He was off in the armed forces,

running through mud and obstacle courses.

That's how I saw it in my mind.

Remember?...that perception thing?

He sent home pictures and presents.

Now I do remember that!

Laughing.

I remember post cards and pictures of him on mountains of snow.

I wanted to go.

I wanted to visit and be with my big bro.

He was so much older though.

And he started a family of his own later.

I babysat his son, my nephew.

He was *my* baby.

I loved him like he was my own.

Even though I wasn't grown.

I was in high school. You know, that school I hate.

Let's not get back on that. Moving on...

    I remember Ellis and my other brother Robert playing outside a lot.

Outside was hot!

Summer was no joke in that valley of a city.

Nope, not pretty.

They had BB guns and shot dragon flies and some other bugs.

Looked like fun.

They also played with our dogs, Pluto and Mercury.

I have to change their names too…ha ha ha!

Even though the dogs are long gone, have to protect them too.

Silly me.

Ellis was cool. He had a big fro

(afro for you non-ethnic folks out there) and played bass guitar.

He listened to a lot of cool music,

Brother's Johnson, Stanley Clarke, Earth Wind and Fire, Bootsy.

He played thump and slap and was as good as any group on any eight-track.

Wow! Eight-track.

I'm old.

Giggling.

      Robert, my other brother I mentioned, and I played together a lot.

Even though he was a boy, it didn't matter because I got

to play with girls' and boys' toys. That was fun.

I would play with my sister, then when I was done,

I played with him and his toys.

He had Tonka trucks and little green Army men,

and Dinky cars made of iron and tin.

I loved playing with him and his toys.

Even though his toys were for boys, I could play too.

My toys weren't nearly as fun.

His army men had fake machine guns,

and they fought mighty battles and every time they won!

I played with his toys, but he didn't play with mine.

No baby dolls and barbies for him.

We fought wars and battles and we would always win.

The bad guys were defeated and we were the winners...

until it was time for dinner.

        He wasn't going to play tea set or paper dolls with me,

so I played with his toys with him. He was very quiet.

If he wasn't playing with the dogs out back, he was in his room.

His time was completely consumed

with fantasy and make believe.

What was he escaping from?

I didn't think of that 'til now.

Maybe it was just how he played.

Children make up fantasy worlds and his were a lot of fun.

We were innocent and young.

Oh yeah, he would also catch frogs or lizards

and bring them in the house and we'd play with them too.

Mama had no idea that's what we would do.

He would make these tiny paper dumbbells or bench press bar or something,

put them in the frogs' hands and put the frogs on their backs and touch their

stomachs. It looked like they were lifting weights.

That was so---- funny!

Those times were great.

I think he used toothpicks and little balled up school paper on the ends for the

weights.

I don't know, but it was fun.

We played most of the day 'til it got late.

I miss that.

        Last but not least, there's Yolanda. She was the closest girl in age to me.

She was both nice and mean to me for some of my childhood.

That was something I never understood, but it was all good.

I found out later it was because she thought I was taking her place.

She didn't know they had enough love to go around.

She had to stand her ground.

She was the baby in the family, NOT me.

She would certainly show me and make me see.

But she wasn't really the baby anyway.

Robert was the youngest but she had to save her place.

Maybe, to her being *the baby* wasn't about age. It was a state of mind, a place in line.

It was about the dynamics of the family.

So she claimed the title of *the baby* and I had to claim the title of *the youngest*.

That never stopped all of my other sisters and brothers from introducing me as *THE BABY* of the family.

Even she would say 'this is my baby sister.'

        Oh! Now I get it! Not *the baby*, but *baby sister*.

That's the difference, and I just got it.

Told you, you learn a lot when you start thinking back.

She and I fought a lot.

I don't think she got mad with each toy that I got.

Because we would also play.

Later she told me she always liked me, loved me, crazy about me.

Back then, that wasn't crystal clear to me. But now it is.

She and I would play paper dolls and barbie dolls and make believe.

I guess it's not just boys who pretend. Girls are good at that.

We image a whole scenario, a whole life, a different world.

We find a cute boy because we're a cute girl.

We get married and have a family.

What is that all about?

Why do girls dream of a family and boys dream of war?

Says a lot, to me.

Do you see what I see? I see a gap.

That's why sometimes we feel trapped.

Trapped in a reality that we didn't dream about.

Anyway, she taught me how to make paper doll clothes

so we could change the doll outfits.

We were designers and didn't even know it.

How about that!

Mama was cool. She made me soup when I was home sick from school.

She taught me how to play cards-- Gin Rummy, Crazy Eights, and even Solitaire.

She and I also played jack stones. I didn't care what it was,

as long as I was playing with her.

She was good!

She never touched any of the other jacks.

And if her jacks were spread out a bit, she was quick.

She scooped them right up.

I think it was just luck.

But I don't think I ever won when I played with her.

She was a great cook too. She could cook anything.

Baked chicken or mashed potatoes and fried chicken wings.

Not just wings; it was all the chicken parts.

That must have been hard.

All that chicken, all those pieces.

Her specialty dinner was steak and rice and gravy.

My sisters and brothers called it 'stankin' rice and gravy'. Chuckle, chuckle.

They were sick of it, but it was still good.

My mama did all she could to make sure we had a great dinner.

        Oh, she baked cakes from scratch!

From scratch I say!

Everyone had their own cake on their birthday.

No matter how many birthdays there were in a month.

A lot of us were born in the same month, but she made each of us our own cake.

Finally, we told her we could just share.

We really didn't care.

Wonder if Yolanda wanted the day to herself.

Guess I can't blame her. Birthdays are important.

I don't mind sharing, but not everyone feels that way.

Anyway, I don't know why mama had so many kids.

Once I asked her why she did.

She really couldn't give me a good answer.

I would have stopped after a couple or maybe three.

Now she probably wishes she had…nah…just kidding.

But see, that's a lot of people to have to worry about.

And my mama is a worrier indeed, without a doubt.

        Some of my sisters and brothers may not think she worries about them, but she does.

What mama couldn't?

What mama wouldn't?

I guess it's because mama's carry their babies inside them,

so close to them.

They're part of them.

They're one.

No matter how mad you may be about something

or how mad you may be at someone,

you still worry if you're a mama.

My mama is strong too.

She's been through a lot and had to do a lot of things

by herself most of the time.

I think it's a crime for a mama to be alone,

taking care of her home and all those kids all on her own.

Shameful!

She's had some surgeries and even survived cancer.

Doc told her she's 'a little piece of leather but well put together'.

And she's still kicking even into her eighties now.

I don't know how.

I guess it's God's blessings.

No, she's not perfect. No one is, and she did the best she knew.

She's only human and humans make mistakes, even you.

I don't understand some of her decisions

and some of her ways of thinking, but like I said,

she did the best she could with what she had.

You gotta respect that, no matter what.

      I can't forget about Daddy,

but by his last name is how he's more known.

His last name is what I call him now that I'm grown.

Everyone who knew him called him either by his last name or by his nickname.

Either way, he's the same man,

A "man"...if you say so. I'll explain later.

I'll refer to him as E.S. for Ellis Sr.

E.S. was my hero when I was young.

I would run to go take off his boots when he would come home.

He was in the armed forces too, but he retired shortly after I was born.

He moved back to the states and made this his home.

He was working somewhere where he still had to wear boots,

but not his armed forces suit.

Just plain clothes.

He looked like he had been working hard from his head to his toes.

He was a little tired, so I would unlace his boots while he sat on the sofa.

His favorite place.

      He always brought me home something.

Nothing much, just some beat up coins.

They were from whatever job he had been on since that morning.

I think mama told me one time what it was, but I don't know.

But I loved when he would walk through that door,

and those old beat up coins were my pride and joy.

Better than any toy.

They were priceless to me because they were each unique,

and because my daddy gave them to me.

I could ask him for anything in the whole wide world.

I was his favorite girl.

He said he would give me the moon if he could.

That's just what a daddy should say to his little girl.

He was my world.

I used to love to count the money in his wallet.

It wasn't a lot but I would count all of it.

I would separate it all by denomination, count it, then stack it all back.

Then start all over. As a matter of fact, I did the same thing with the coins.

It was silly, but it was fun.

And I could ask him for anything.

If I asked for $20, he would give it to me.

I was 5 or 6 so I didn't need money,

but I just wanted to ask and have my daddy give it to me.

Later on, he would ask for it back, and I would give it to him.

I didn't really want it anyway. I just wanted something from him.

Why? I have no idea.

I'm sure some psychiatrist could come up with some super deep explanation for it. But I think it's simple.

I just liked playing with money.

Still do a little bit. Hee hee.

    So that's my peeps.

We were all in the house together...except my oldest sister...

and all doing whatever it was we did all day.

Needless to say,

I was probably playing with either Robert or Yolanda and if not,

then I was playing with my chalk board and chalk.

Something was always keeping me busy.

I was a happy kid.

No reason not to be, so I did whatever kids do.

With that happy family, wouldn't you?

The dogs were outside chasing birds or squirrels, or whatever dogs do.

Kitty, the cat, was somewhere in the house doing what cats do too.

He came out now and then but wasn't out a lot that I can remember.

He either died later or mama gave him away.

I just know he was here one day then gone the next day.

But he was fun to play with.

Before the guinea pig died, he would be in his cage,

or me or my brother had him out playing with him.

He had a good life too, before he died.

Delia was probably listening to her music with LeShae
They shared a room and were in it most of the day.
Mama was watching her soap operas or doing "mama stuff" around the house,
and daddy was probably at work or if he was home,
he was stretched out on the couch watching TV.
We were all one big happy family,
or at least that's how it seemed to me.
I couldn't imagine it any other way.
Every day, each day the same sort of play.
Kind of routine, but it was cool to me.
I guess that's what middle class families do.
They have their set ways and are pretty much set in them too.
It was good.
I was good.

Christmas was always fun, and we always had a ton of toys and food
and everything tasted so good!
We had tons of fruit and different kinds of nuts...brazil, walnut, pecan.
Mama would cook these huge meals and we would eat all we can.
It was more food than I could ever want.
I had tons of toys, toys for girls but not for boys.
Boys' toys were for the boys...back in the day anyway.
I don't know why but it was ok.
Seemed like the whole Christmas tree was nothing but toys for me.
I know everyone else got stuff too,
but I felt like I was opening gifts all morning.
It was great.
All holidays were great but Christmas was extra special.
We always had a live tree...at least as far as I can remember.

Daddy would cut the bottom and put a little sugar water in the stand.

That was supposed to keep the tree fresh longer, so it would last.

Or maybe it was mama who put the sugar water in the stand.

I don't know, but we had a live tree and it smelled great.

Even to this day, the smell of a fresh Christmas tree is special to me.

The house smelled like Christmas. I can't describe it in a word.

Christmas was ham, turkey, dressing, collards, macaroni and cheese, cornbread, sweet potato pie, pound cake and we could eat as much as we please.

Oh my goodness! It was special.

We always had traditional Christmas food.

It was so---- good!

When I was little, there never seemed to be an end to it.

How did my mama do it?

She cooked all that from scratch.

No boxed food for her, and no chef was a match for my mama's cooking.

And we had leftovers. Leftovers?

With so many people in the house?

I don't know how my mama managed that.

My mama was a magician!

And Christmas was MAJIC!

      I had cool grandparents.

Grandma and Granddaddy would come to visit sometimes.

I don't know how my mama found the time to take care of all of us,

never put up a fuss,

never cuss,

and still entertain her parents.

I guess it's a must if you're a mama.

Grandma would take a quarter out of her change purse...

they still used change purses back then...

and give it to me.

Put the biggest grin on my face

and on her face too, to see me smiling so big and happy.

She had a way of hugging and kissing you that was warm and loving.

She squeezed you tight.

Kissed you on the cheek not once, but twice.

      We would go visit them sometimes too and when we did,

Granddaddy would give me a coca cola in the glass bottle all to myself.

I don't remember him doing that for anybody else.

It seemed so big to me because I was so small.

Mama didn't let me have soda at home at all,

so this was a special treat.

I would sit at the kitchen table swinging my feet.

They didn't touch the floor. Still don't. Ha-ha!

I played with my cousins outside either in the back yard on the front porch.

If we were in back, I was on the swing set.

If we were in the front, I was picking honey suckle flowers and eating the sweet drops. Or maybe Grandma had some pomegranates or half an orange she would give me.

I was happy at home and at Grandma's.

They were safe places to be.

I was loved and life was good;

at least it was good to me.

I guess that was all I could really see.

I was a kid and not really seeing anything other than what I did.

Who pays attention to a lot when they are just a kid.

Now I wish I did.

I wish I paid attention to all the little things.

Instead, I just saw things my childish way.

Innocent.

Loving.

Secure.

Free.

Happy.

What's wrong with that you say?

I guess it's delusional. You need to know better.

But maybe later.

For now, just be a kid and be happy.

Don't take that away. Not now. Not yet.

I bet if you could go back in time, you would find a way to make it last longer.

Your innocence.

Your fun.

Your happy times.

Like the ones you remember when you think back,

to what you were doing, and what you were eating,

and who you were with, and even what you could smell,

when a particular song came out...

"Tell Me If You Still Care", "Love Overboard", "Thriller", "Benny and the Jets",

"Sweet Home Alabama", "Love Hangover", "Pink Cadillac", "Bernadette",

"Make My Funk the P Funk", "Endless Love", "Sweet Caroline",

"My Girl", "Billie Jean", "Living for the City", "Ribbon in the Sky".

Yeah you know what I'm talking about...I know you remember.

It's nostalgia.

It's heaven.

It's safe.

It's childhood all over again.

Wish I could go back. Back before things became so twisted.

So different. So wrong.

So long.

Goodbye happiness. "Good Morning Heartache". Shout out Natalie Cole.

Chapter 3: When?

When did it all start?

One night we left and went to Grandma's.

I had been to her house many times before,

so going wasn't a big deal anymore.

But this time it was at night.

Something wasn't right.

We usually went during the day but didn't stay.

Now we were spending the night.

It was dark and we were settling in, finding places to sleep.

It wasn't normal, but I didn't think too much of it at the time.

It was time to just sleep. Have peace.

A couple days later, I asked mama when we were going back.

She didn't really have anything to say to that.

I don't remember what she actually said,

but the thought was going through my head that I missed my own bed.

But she didn't tell me we were going back.

I don't know if she knew what she was really going to do,

but going back at this time wasn't what she had in mind.

I can't image she thought this was where we were going to stay.

Everyday?

No, because she left all my toys at home and didn't bring anything with us.

She can't really be serious!

She couldn't possibly have planned on staying and making this home.

My teddy bear was all alone.

He missed me and I missed him,

and the dinky cars, and trucks,

and the chalk and chalk board,

and tea set and paper dolls, and paper doll clothes.

She wouldn't dare leave them behind at all.

No we were definitely going to go home,

or else she would have let me bring my toys along.

The next day came and we didn't go home.

The next day came and we were still gone.

The next day came and we started getting bunk beds in my aunt's room.

The next day came and now Thanksgiving was coming soon.

We must have been there for a month and it must now have been December

because Christmas was right around the corner.

Christmas at Grandma's?

Would it be like Christmas at home?

Would there be collards, and macaroni and cheese,

and all the toys we could possibly need?

Would the tree be alive and have sugar water in the stand?

Would the food be endless and we could eat all the food that we can?

NO!

Their tree had all these spider web looking things on it.

They felt like spider webs too. 'Angel hair', mama said.

Why would they do that to a Christmas tree?

Spider webs are for Halloween.

This is the **worst** Christmas tree I've ever seen!

I was scared of how it felt on my skin.

I would **NOT** get my presents from under that tree.

Oh no! Not me!

Mama had to get them. I wasn't going anywhere near them.

And it was **NOT** a live tree!

It didn't smell like Christmas, not exactly.

Yes Grandma cooked a Christmas dinner, but I don't think we ate any of it.
At least not that I remember ...or was that Thanksgiving..I don't know
Instead, my brother Ellis went to Church's Chicken,
and that's what we had for our supper.
My grandma called it supper, not dinner.
I didn't like the Church's Chicken meat but I liked the skin. So I traded mine in.
Traded with my brother Robert for his chicken skin.
Surely Grandma must have offered us dinner and mama just said 'no thank you'.
I don't remember, but I can't imagine Grandma not offering.
I'm not sure why mama said no thank you. Maybe she was being polite.
There was not a lot of food in sight,
so maybe she didn't want to be rude.
She taught us to be polite and not take something from other people
if they don't have a lot.
Maybe that's why she said no thank you....being polite.
I guess that's right.
From then on, things with Grandma, Granddaddy, and my cousins were
different.
No big coca cola.
No quarters from change purses.
I don't know why, but it just wasn't the same like
when they came to our house or we went to theirs.
Maybe because they came and then left.
We were staying.
      What was happening?
What was going on?
We were there for so long?
It seemed an eternity. Where was my daddy?

I called and we talked on the phone.

On the phone?

Why am I reduced to a phone call?

I used to have a home…with my daddy and his boots and his beat up coins.

Where did things go wrong?

I don't understand. "Mama, can we go home?"

"Daddy, can we come home?

Why won't you come pick us up?

When are you coming to see me again?"

Silence….no one can answer my questions.

I'm sad…

        Okay, okay. You're going to be okay.

That's what I would say.

But there were bugs and the bathroom smelled funny.

It smelled 'old man funny'.

I never noticed it before. When they would visit me or I would visit them.

I never smelled it then.

Now I'm smelling 'old man smell'.

Not stinky, just old man smell.

I can't tell where the smell is coming from. It's just smelly.

One bathroom in the whole house!

My aunt and her kid, Grandma and Granddaddy,

my mama, my sisters Delia and Yolanda, and me,

my brother Robert and my uncles, two of them I think.

That's too many people for one bathroom.

Seems funny how it seemed like enough room though.

Never had to wait in line to pee.

Don't know how we made it work. But we did.

I don't remember a lot 'cause I was just a little kid.

But it wasn't really that bad, at least not for me.

But I still missed my dad, but it wasn't too bad.

After Christmas was over and the spider webs were gone,

I was okay with this being our new home....for now.

    My grandma was sweet. She gave us all slices of oranges to eat.

My cousins chewed until the juice was gone,

then spit out the pulp in my grandma's palm.

They were just toddlers so they couldn't chew and swallow the pulp and skin.

I was a bigger kid so I ate it all.

They sat in her lap.

I was too big for that, so I sat on the floor next to her.

She was so sweet. Always smiling at me.

Hugs and kisses for everyone.

They had a nice home. I guess. But it still wasn't mine.

Plus my aunt and my sister Yolanda argued some of the time.

That's not what my mama taught us.

'Respect your elders' is what mama said.

But the idea got in my sister's head

that my aunt was not the boss of her.

Yolanda could say what she wanted.

My aunt didn't like that at all.

Tried to smack my sister once.

Where was mama? I don't remember.

But don't get it twisted,

I don't have no punk for a sister.

She not gonna get slapped or even grabbed at.

Mess with her and you better get back.

'Smack me and I'll smack you back'. Shout out Digital Underground.

So it was on.

We were in my aunt's home and she wasn't gonna have it.

My sister better respect her.

My sister pissed off my aunt one time.

They went back and forth...seemed always to taunt each other.

I think my aunt told her daughter not to go near Yolanda.

But my cousin loved her and was crazy about my sister.

My sister was pretty and nice to my cousin.

My sister tried to stay away from my cousin one day.

Cousin cried like a baby.

My sister must have thought maybe this isn't a good idea.

Didn't like my cousin's crocodile tears.

She had to go back. Forget what my aunt said.

This was a child so while we were there,

my sister wouldn't dare be mean. No reason to be.

It seemed silly to ignore a sweet kid.

So from then on, my sister never did.

My sister loved my cousin,

and my cousin loved my sister.

        But where was my sister mama, mama sister?

At some point I missed her not being there.

But actually, she was gone

long before we ever stepped foot through my grandma's door.

LeShae moved out or was put out. Where was she now?

I saw her sometimes.

She made me a teddy bear since my other teddy got left behind...

at my *real* home.

She made it for me so I wouldn't be alone.

This is my favorite toy now.

Finally my mama moved out. Got her own house.

Thank God!

A place of our own. We would make this our new home.

Gotta get some new toys to take the place of the others.

But not my sister mama's. My teddy bear is near and dear to my heart.

Never will we ever part. It's part of me now.

      I guess I need to back up a little bit again.

Pardon the incongruence.

It's a lot to tell, so bear with me while I work through it.

Ok, here we go... way back before, when daddy was still coming home.

One night he came home late and at first it was alright.

I was in the kitchen and he came through the door.

I jumped up in his arms like I had done so many times before.

But it was different this time. I felt something uncomfortable, out of line.

I don't know what it was, but when he was holding me up,

there was something uncomfortable, hands in the wrong place.

Violating my space.

My heart was numb.

Why didn't I wiggle or squirm or move out of the way?

What would he say?

Mama was standing right there. Did she know?

I don't think so.

She couldn't know because I didn't say a word.

I just looked and sat quiet like a 'good little girl'.

I should have said something.

Say something.

Say something!

Tell!

TELL!

Don't just let this happen!

He must not know what he was doing. I was his kid.

No. It was a mistake.

But wait...

can't you tell when something's out of place.

Like when you slip your shoes on the wrong foot

or socks twisted round and toes not in the right toe spot.

Oh no. He had to know.

I was so uncomfortable. More uncomfortable than I ever had been before.

Silent, I sat, waiting for him to put me down.

Sad, uncomfortable, scared.

Mama, can't you see my face?

There's no expression.

Can't you see something is wrong?

Of course she can't tell because I don't tell.

I feel so alone. Mama had no clue.

I didn't know what to do.

Is this why my sister kept me so close?

To keep me from the monster that she had already gotten to know.

Is this why my sister left before we did?

No, she was just a kid.

She was his kid too. What do I do?

Oh God, show me what to do!

       Just then, he put me down and I run off.

I don't remember where I went.

Anywhere but here. Gotta get out of this place.

Find me a safe space.

No. I had to tell myself that it was mistake.

My daddy loved me too much to do anything like that to me. But he did.

No he didn't. You misunderstood.

He wasn't up to no good.

His hands were numb from all that car crushing or whatever he did to get those beat up coins.

It was nothing.

He didn't mean it.

It didn't happen.

Put it out of your mind.

Forget and never remember.

The mind is a funny thing. Things that are too traumatic for us to handle get pushed down deep into the hidden archives.

You forget all about it.

It didn't happen.

You were dreaming.

It disappears.

All your tears and fears erased.

Like chalk on a chalk board. But even then there's some residue left behind.

Just waiting for someone to come in and find a trace,

a hint, not clear but still slightly there.

So one day, when you least expect it, yeah you guessed it.

It comes back from the archives to the forefront. Something brings it back.

Some completely unrelated event, totally not related to it, happens.

Then in a flash, like a camera flash, or like when a light bulb blows out...

quick, bright for a split second then dark again.

A hint of what happened way back when.

It gets pulled back out from God only knows where.

Out of thin air...

you remember.

Oh my God!

Did that really happen to me? Was it a dream or reality?

It couldn't be. But then the physical recall kicks in,

and you start to remember way back when.

You remember the feeling first, not the details.

Then slowly but surely, the details from that erased chalk board become clear.

I remember like it was yesterday.

I had on a red robe with white lace boxed around the collar.

Probably only cost a few dollars

but it was special to me.

I felt like a princess in my robe...royalty.

It was as long as a gown. All the way down to my toes.

It was like satin and kind of quilted.

Maybe that's why daddy didn't feel it.

Didn't feel it because his hands were too numb.

Had no feelings in his fingers or thumb.

Naw.

He knew.

Had to know.

I don't know.

I can't say for sure but I can't see how he couldn't.

My mama was right there but had no clue.

Mama was the one protecting me from the witch in my dreams.

She would have protected me from him if she knew.

I didn't tell her then. I should have told her way back when.

But I did later.

It was a long time later but I finally told her. And there she was...**the witch**.

Is she here to torment me again? I thought I beat her up and cussed her out.

Scrunched up face looking all ugly and twisted and frowned up hard.

Oh my God!

Good God! What is mama about to say?

Why is her face scrunched up that way...like the witch?

As fast as the lightning strikes in the sky,

crazy thoughts raced through my mind.

Will she fuss at me for saying something so horribly wrong about my dad?

Will she say,

'That didn't happen to you! He didn't do what you said.

That's all in your head.

Or maybe you heard someone else talking about that one day.

You're remembering it the wrong way?

It wasn't you. He never did that to you.'

Or will she say,

'Oh God, my poor baby!

No!

I'm so sorry. I didn't know.

I will chase him away right now, you know how...like I did that witch'.

Son of a b---....

No! I have to get you out of this place.

Gotta get out of this place.

Find you a safe space.

He's a disgrace to men.'

Which will it be? Will she cuss at me or hug me and tell me she's sorry and loves me?

Now I know who the witch is.

The witch is denial and pain and regret and shame

and resentment and guilt and sadness.

The witch is all the missed signs and all the good times

you thought that you had, but you hadn't.

The witch is helplessness, that feeling you get

when you thought you were safe, but you weren't.

The witch is powerlessness and pain in your chest

and all the world's greatest hurt.

My mama was sad.

A kind of sadness you can't even begin to imagine.

I think the same witch who was chasing me was chasing my mama now.

I could tell by the look in her eyes…she looked terrorized.

Just the way I felt in my dreams.

I want to scream.

Scream!

Scream and let it all out!

No, that would hurt my mama even more, no doubt.

Her face went solemn, plain, her arms dropped to her side.

She didn't cry, she just sat, silent, quiet, alone,

like she was numb all over and her face was numb too.

The scrunched up witch face was gone.

Mama's mind must have chased it away.

Remember me saying things that are too traumatic for us to handle

get pushed down deep into the hidden archives?

Well, mama's mind must have pushed this down for herself this time.

Hey, I just figured out what the closed door meant.

You know...the door that closes right before the witch comes?

It represents the closed mind.

Your mind is trying to close out the pain.

Trying to erase the shame.

Trying to survive. There's more to this but I need to leave it behind.

I don't want to hurt mama so now's not the time to get into it.

I know mama means well.

I also know right now she's catching hell. Shout out Natalie Cole.

So I keep quiet just like I did when I was a kid...

in my daddy's arms, in harm's way.

That's probably why I was quiet all those other times...

when the other boys and men hurt me later down the line.

They were just another representation of my daddy.

No, not daddy.

He's his last name to me now.

Don't know how I can ever call him daddy again...

now that I remember what he did to me

when I was just a little kid way back then.

I think *that's* the real *when* of this chapter.

When that happened, it shaped my lack of trust in men from then on.

When that happened, it shut my eyes and jaded my soul.

When that happened, it broke me down to a damaged, little, withered flower.

Still a flower, but withered.

Sad...droopy...needing some sunlight...needing some water...needing a new father.

The only father I have now is my Father in heaven.

Save me Lord.

Chapter 4: Where?

Back to where I left off earlier. Where would I go next?

I transferred college thinking it would be better just to be somewhere else.

Why back home though? Didn't I have enough of a bad experience there?

But I did it anyway. I met a nice young man one day.

He was kind and seemed to have it together.

Worked in the mall...not too terribly tall but then neither was my father.

I was short so his height was definitely no bother for me.

We were great together. Finally got around to being really close.

I was pretty much ok with it by then. Didn't mean anything anymore.

But with him it was different.

Special.

So we did.

But oh my God what happened next was nothing I would have ever been prepared for.

I found myself not just one anymore.

He was not happy with that.

Told me he would fight and take everything away from me.

He wanted to put an end to it.

What!?

Are you crazy?

Didn't I try to stay away from murder at that college, with that other boyfriend when I was drunk and in his room playing with the pocket knife, wanting so badly to take his life but didn't because I didn't want to break one of the big ten?

Whew!

That's a lot to say in one breath.

But yet here I was, taking that step.

One of *the reals* went with me.

She was discrete.

I kept it hidden from everyone. Was a long time before I finally told mama.

Back then, she had a bad way of saying things.

Like if you were intimate, you were 'running around with men'.

That's a bad way to put what could be such a beautiful experience...

with the right person... your husband.

It made you feel low, lower than low.

Yet there I go, there I go, there I go...shout out James Moody...

telling her about it anyway.

She actually handled it pretty well. Why not?

See, one of my sisters had already spilled the beans.

I don't remember how it came about, but she figured it out...

or so she thought she did.

I told her a different story so now she was sorry she mentioned it to my mama.

A little bit of drama, but now the real story was out.

My mama was ok though.

No scrunched up witch face this time.

      Anyway, I did what I did. Never spoke about it again,

but was always talking about leaving this world.

One of my friends caught on and asked why I was always saying stuff like that.

She knew too. Knew what I had done. At some point I told her.

She was cool though. She could relate.

For decades I felt like I let God down.

I was horrible and not worth being here or worth His love.

I still loved Him but didn't love myself

or forgive myself so how could anybody else?...

even God?

For Him it had to be hard...

with so many children to look after and each one being hard headed

not following your rules. You would get mad at them too.

But like a mama loves her kids, He still loves His kids too.

Thank God!

Thank *You* God.

        Going where now? Meet another great guy.

Ok, it's been bad in the past, but I'll give it one more try. This time it will last.

He wants to marry me.

I'm carrying his seed.

I told him about the time before. He threw it up in my face one day.

Blew me away!

Something I told you in confidence about my circumstance

that almost took me from this place and you throw it in my face?

Really?

Wow!

What a jerk!

But he didn't mean it that way.

He thought I was going to do the same thing.

He was just trying to let me know he didn't want me or baby to go.

"Oh"

Wow

After all the other dumb brothers, I thought for a second, he was just another.

No.

He wanted to get married…to me.

Me!

Little old me who was only half way through college,

part time job, and now gonna be a mom.

Yes me!

So we set out to find the justice of the peace.

Wouldn't you know it? They moved from where they used to be.

'Maybe God is trying to tell you something?' Shout out Color Purple.

He was also in the armed forces and a war was about to start.

It took us apart. Broke my heart.

But we wrote each other every day.

Always had something new to say.

Never a dull moment. Sometimes he would call too.

I was so excited. He always reassured me he loved me.

Couldn't wait to be a daddy.

He told me that where he was, there were no women around.

But then one day he mentioned a spider came out

and scared this woman in their work tent. He said he had to kill it.

Guess he forgot he told me there were no women around before. Hmmph!

Now the letters were a little different. Each one he sent seemed more distant.

'I'm feeling lethargic' he says.

Oh, so you learned a new word?

That's absurd.

Too late now. Baby's on the way soon.

You buffoon!

No, I don't say that. As always, I'm quiet.

Don't yell, don't scream, don't put on a scene.

Don't cry, don't sigh, don't even try.

No. I write back and give him an out. I tell him I'm okay with not getting married.

And I really am, honestly. I just want him to be a good dad.

That was what I wish I had. A good dad.

And he was nothing like my dad. He was a good dad.

Thank God!

But still, baby's gonna be in a broken home too.

My baby, my son.

Sad face...sigh...cry...

    So he's back in town, we're ok...not really together but not really apart.

Still a broken heart though. Where do we go from here?

South out Johnny Gill and Stacy Lattisaw ...or is it Lattimore? I don't know.

Well it's back to class I go I guess.

Keep on moving and forget about the rest.

I was in the middle of college when all this transpired.

I was always tired.

But everything is going okay, then I'm walking along one day

on campus and all of sudden I see a last name.

One in the same as baby's daddy, but this ain't baby's daddy's body.

It's a little hottie...or so she thought.

She was strutting like a peacock. His name on the back of the shirt of some girl?

My mind went into a whirl.

What?! Naw, that's not...what??!!

I followed her to make sure I saw what I was seeing.

I'm not believing my eyes. I don't even cry this time. At least not yet.

    So baby is here and not even two weeks have passed

and this sorry behind man has someone wearing his name?

I roll up at the residence to see what's going on. I knock, door opens, he steps outside.

Now that's a new one...total surprise.

What? I can't come inside?

Never happened before.

Oh now you got something to hide?

Someone's inside?

Oh you gotta be kidding me?

Is this the same chick I saw with your name?

One in the same!

I was supposed to be wearing your ring, and now you do this thing?

Having a fling?

Or is this for real?

'I'm having dinner' he says.

"Lights are off in the house. How you having dinner?"

'I have company.'

"Oh you do, do you?"

My mind whirls again. What about us, what about baby? What about your son?

Do I kill him and this trick?

Yes? No? Maybe so?

Scrunched up witch face is back.

Except this time it's on *my* face!

Humiliation, shame, disgrace.

Gotta get out of this place.

I'm still with stitches and these trick ass bitch is doing this crap?

Oh...forgot I wasn't supposed to cuss anymore. Forgive me Lord.

But I'm pissed. I'm upset to say the least. My worst nightmare!

Another daddy not with the mama.

Too much drama.

Okay, okay.

You're going to be okay.

This is what I say to myself but inside I'm crying, dying, trying to hold back the tears.

But they flow.

Harder and louder than ever before.

I can't believe this is happening. Baby is in a broken home.

Just like my home, but thank God this daddy isn't a psycho, sick-o, sadistic, sucker.

Nevertheless, I'm all alone.

Me and baby are all alone.

I can't do this on my own.

But I'm strong. I *can* make it on my own.

I'm on my own. Shout out Patty Labelle and Michael McDonald.

Driving back home and I'll be darn, Jodeci, Forever My Lady comes on.

No joke! I ain't lying.

I couldn't make this crap up even if I was trying.

At that moment, at that exact time, the darn song came on.

You ever cried and laughed at the same time?

So there I am, single mom just like my mama, raising a son by myself.

My man left. Put my love in a jar to rot away on a shelf.

At least my mama was married at first. Married to her man before her baby's birth….well…the second baby anyway…remember the sister with a different last name?

But not me. I'm a baby mama, not a wife.

This is now my life.

Do you know he actually called me one day? ..my baby daddy.

He actually asked me if I would get back together with him.

Can you believe that? What is that?

Is that what I want?

He has my heart doing summersaults.

Why does he taunt me with this proposal?

He proposed before, but we never made it through that door, never said "I do" before.

So don't get it twisted. I keep up my guard.

I guard my heart.

He may be pulling another bait and switch.

I think he knew where the justice of the peace was that day. That was part of his play.

Set, hut one, hut two, hut three, hike.

Throw a pass and pass by the justice of the peace

and pretend you don't see it right down the street.

That's what I found out later.

It was down the street, but we turned the corner too soon...by accident or on purpose? I don't know.

I have no peace with being a baby mama but still, I guard my heart.

"Hell no! You just be a good dad."

Why did I say that?

I should have jumped at the chance to give my son a chance to have a happy family...

like the one I thought I had.

Should have given it a try though. But yet I deny him a chance to have a mama and a dad.

Sad...

    Baby's growing up, and now we need a new place.

Gotta get out of this place.

Need a new space.

So off to the next town I go.

Somewhere where there's no one I know.

Except my new boyfriend lives in the state next door.

Ha ha ha! Ok, here we go...

It's not so bad. He's a good man, but guess what!

He's in the armed forces too.

First daddy...I mean the man with the last name,

then baby daddy,

now new boyfriend...all in the armed forces.

Is he gonna be the same disappointment, same kind of time spent running in circles?

You got me going in circles, round and round I go. Shout out Friends of Distinction.

Have I become a slave to the insanity of dating and waiting

on someone to love me for real?

I just want to feel love...real love, the kind that lasts forever. Shout out Lakeside.

    I need to go inside myself

and find love on the inside of me

before I can expect anyone else to see

that I deserve what I'm looking for,

searching for,

desperate for.

But no,

I ignore this common sense because I have no sense of self,

of self-worth,

of the fact that I had a right from birth

to be loved and respected and not neglected.

I continue this path of self-destruction not even knowing that's what it is.

New boyfriend breaks my heart.

Cheated...but not really...or so he says.

One day he went on a trip and let it slip that he was with another woman...

oh...but "nothing happened".

Yeah right!

Ok, next.

So I meet a sexy, chocolate, delectable, delicious, tall drink of water.

He had a mother and father raise him so he should be ok.

Wait...but so did most if not all of the others.

So that makes no difference obviously.

Does that mean my son will be ok with just me as a single mom?

If others who had mom and dad were no different from those who had just a mom,

will baby be ok?

Good God! I hope he will be better than all of them.

Of course he will.

I'm raising him, so I will make sure I raise a good man.

That's the promise I made God when I found out baby was coming.

Anyway, sexy chocolate (shout out Coming to America) is a good man, good job, nice house, no crazy history of women.

Uh oh...hold up!

Conversation brings revelation of a situation that is haunting this nation.

Living together?

He's actually *living together* with his ex.

Is she really an 'ex' or is it just *'some on the side'* for the next time you need a quick fix?

His *live-in's* mom works with me so I get all the gossip.

You see, she tells me things that he doesn't know about

so I'm not in the dark and I can figure out

what my next step is. I got this. I'm calling the shots.

I feel like The Wiz (shout out)...Red, Green, Golden Gold!

I'm not gonna sell my soul to this one.

You either gonna poo or get off the pot.

Give an ultimatum.

That'll make him do what he's supposed to do. Ha ha! Yeah right! Think again.

That's wrong, he's gone.

Gave me a gift before he left too.

Had to go get a shot.

Guess *live in* wasn't just a '*live in*'.

She was '*some on the side*'. Pissed!!!

    New boyfriend…what is this…'bout number 10 now? I lost count.

Ok so new boyfriend also has a kid and he's cool.

Moved his mom in with him to look out for her too.

She's got a minor health issue, but the real issue is that if she lives with him,

it's her house…no matter who's paying the mortgage.

She's the woman of the house and without a doubt

she's gonna treat him like when he used to live in her house.

I tried to warn him, but he didn't believe me…until it happened…over and over.

Nevertheless, she was cool with me.

I liked her and we could talk and hang out and walk around the mall and go

shopping.

I don't know if new boyfriend liked that very much.

His son liked me too.

Thought I was supposed to be his girlfriend too…that's cute.

One big happy family.

Me, my son, new boyfriend number 10,11,12…whatever,

and his son…all together.

But what makes me think this time there won't be stormy weather?

Shout out Ethel Waters.

    Sunshine in the morning with a light morning dew.

That's what love feels like when it's new.

Rainbows and butterflies over my head.

That's what I see when I lay in your bed.

Songs of love sung in my head.

That's what I hear when we're hand in hand.

This one is going to last.

But then comes a dark cloud of gray. Words we never would normally say, we say.

Broken promises and tear stains.

Daggers are shot through the heart giving love a bad name. Shout out Bon Jovi.

Yes, stormy weather is sure to come.

You can't get around it, but can you stand the rain? Shout out New Edition.

I couldn't stand it and neither could he, so we part ways and once again,

I'm lonely.

Sad...too bad...

    'Heaven please send, to all mankind,

understanding and peace of mind,

but if it's not asking too much,

please send me someone to love.' Shout out Sade.

I used to play it over and over. I knew every note, every tone.

Yes I knew that song well. I feel her pain because mine is the same.

So God hears my prayers and sends me a good ol' big ol' country boy.

He actually proposes, but I should have seen the signs.

He wanted to play house, live together. to make sure he was "gonna be okay with it", is what he said.

Like a fool I fall for it.

Go along with it.

Now I hate it.

Never should have done it.

But I did. A year of my life wasted.

A year wasted for me and my kid. But this was supposed to be different.

I was supposed to be this boyfriend's wife.

Gotta get out of this place.

Once again find me a new space.

New boyfriend again and there seems to be no end to the mess, lies, disguise.

He said he was divorced, but, of course, I didn't ask to see the *blue backed paper*.

I should have demanded it.

But no, once again, I'm silent.

Now I'm crying.

Pissed.

Mad as hell.

But who can I blame but myself?

Next is a young'en that I thought would be different.

I thought he would like an older woman. He did for a minute.

Next one seems like a good match. Seems like a nice catch.

Met him through family. Seemed perfect for me.

It started out just as a mutual attraction. Turned into sweet satisfaction.

He was good to me. There for me. Wanted to be near me.

Wanted to make me happy.

We both had a fling on the side that was our *Mr and Miss out of town*,

but they were nothing to us, and we were special to each other.

So I thought we were going to drop *Mr and Miss out of town*

and make it around to just him and me.

Sad to see those greeting cards on the table from *Miss out of town*.

This is no *Miss out of town*.

This is real! Now I feel like a home wrecker.

She's head-over-heels in love with this man.

He said she's just a friend (shout out Biz Markie)

but he's more to her and she's more to him than he's telling me.

What is he telling her?

Does she even know I exist?

This is the twist.

I met his whole family...

kids, mama, sister, brother, cousins, aunts, uncles...the whole gang.

But check this out.

He and *Miss out of town* have been going on family trips together.

He and his kids, she and hers, all together like the freaking Brady Bunch!

I see pictures...can't remember where I saw them, but I see pictures.

They look like they're having fun. Sun of a gun!

These cards aren't just sweet, they're deep.

She's head-over-heels and I feel like a fool again.

Oh, he says 'you know I have feelings for you'...yes he said that!

Ok, possible to love more than one person at the same time.

I know I'm a lotta woman, but not enough to divide the pie. Shout out Eryka Badu.

So I gotta get out of this place. Gotta find me a new space.

Gotta quit this rat race.

Gotta stop being a disgrace to my family and to my faith and to me.

I gotta find some peace.

I drop him and let it go because deep down inside I know this will never be.

I've done too much of this boyfriend thing.

Time to just do me. Time to set my mind free.

Time to go back to who I know I'm supposed to be.

That little girl standing on top of the table shouting out "I---!"

and rocking my hips from side to side.

Chapter 5: How?

How did I end up here? With so many failures and so many tears?

By now I guess you figured it out. Broken home, daddy left me alone,

pain from things that went wrong. Every story doesn't go like this.

So don't miss the point and think it's all about the circumstance.

Yes, they play a big part. But after a few years and adulthood,

shouldn't I have understood that all this was on me.

I have a mind, a voice.

I can say yes or no.

I have a choice.

What I choose to do can't be put on you. Or can it?

I don't know. Ask a psychiatrist. I certainly don't understand it.

But how I ended up here shaped what was to come.

How I ended up here is how I finally let go of it all.

Ding dong the witch is dead! Shout out Wizard of Oz.

Not everyone is going to relate, appreciate, they may even berate me for this

chapter.

But I don't care. I'm free. I've been set free.

'Therefore, if the Son makes you free, you shall be free indeed' John 8:36 (NKJV).

I'm gonna tell it and if you can't handle it, then close the book and move on.

But if you want to know about the real love of my life,

the final boyfriend, the one that really did make me his wife,

the one that made the hurt all gone, then read on baby, read on.

Baby is not a baby anymore. He's all grown up now.

Managed to turn out pretty darn good despite the broken home situation.

I'm a proud mom.

Oh yeah, we had our set of issues. What mom and kid don't?

But I kept kiddo from the craziness of my life as much as I could.

I may have been overprotective. That's what kiddo says.

I got out of that place and moved to a new space.

New space in my heart,

new space in my mind,

new space this time,

where I was at peace with me

and all I could see around me.

That's when I met him. The day after the move.

Did the earth move?

I don't know, but he definitely had his own groove.

Smooth.

Seductive.

Sexy mother...shut your mouth. Shout out Shaft.

Yeah...he was nice.

But by now my heart was guarded, my perception of men was jaded,

shade had been left on my sunny day.

I can't *begin* to say how *much* I wanted it to be real,

but yet I can't help but feel there's something I should watch out for.

Where's that other proverbial shoe?

What's his angle?

What's he trying to do?

       I hesitate out of fear. I don't want to hear 'I love you' again if it's not real.

Two weeks go by and I don't know why, but he asked and I gave him my number.

Actually told him my middle name...the one that only family calls me.

What?

What is this?

I'm letting him in?

All the others called me by my school name.

You know back then when I was a kid, they didn't ask you what your 'preferred name' is.

They called you by your first name. So that's how everyone outside of family knew me.

But not him.

I let him into a world that no man had gone before. Shout out Star Trek.

But I'm still watching my back.

And he's a writer so he knows all the good lines to say, lies to tell,

stories to make up, big dreams to sell.

Make me sell my soul. Oh no. You won't get me caught up.

So I keep my guard up.

He has an ulterior motive.

I just know it.

        But he never shows it. I don't see it. Can't believe it.

Next thing I know he's talking about marriage and being a family.

How can this be? He wants to marry me?

Me with the *fitty-levem* (you gotta be from the country to know that word) boyfriends?

Me with the past full of sin?

Me with the baby daddy?

Me with the dad whose last name I used instead of daddy?

Naw, this can't be.

He's up to something.

I know it.

Time will show it.

But for now, I'll go along with it. He's given me no reason so far not to.

A few months pass and we're picking out rings.

I've done the same thing before,

so this isn't necessarily the final stop on the boyfriend express.

We'll see if he passes the test.

Mama has to meet him. Big sister too.

You know, the oldest one from the house...the one I wanted to be like.

I'll see what they say and that'll let me know what to do.

Wow!

They like him too.

My sister even invites me and him to dinner.

But something happens that rubs her the wrong way.

She's damaged too so I don't pay her no nevermind that day.

I keep it moving and keep on my way.

I'm glad I didn't listen because it was nothing at all. Shout out Heart.

    Mama gave him the thumbs up.

Now if *she* can like a man, then he *must* be a good one.

She don't like NO MAN.

Her man...the man whose last name I call instead of dad...

broke her heart into a million pieces.

So if she can put it back together...back together just a little bit...

a little bit to let someone love her daughter without putting up a fit...

then he must be a good one.

'Cause no man under the son was ever good enough for her baby.

There was one she tried to warn me about...

well...she did that with all of them...but one in particular...

she warned me that if he was asking me all the time where I was going,

it was because he wanted to make sure he didn't run into me

when he was out doing *his* dirt.

Dang if she wasn't right!

I caught this fool out one night...red handed with a red-head.

Tried to beat his behind dead. But I drove away and didn't kill nobody that day.

Glad I didn't break a top ten. Chuckles.

So anyway, mama and big sis approve.

This is the right move and I found my new groove.

He's kind and sweet and loves little ol' me.

The same me who got lunch for free.

The same me with fake friends that lied on me.

The same me that had a dad who didn't love me.

The same me who had too many boyfriends in my history.

The same me with a grown-up kid and a baby daddy.

Yes, me!

But see, first I had to learn to love me. That's the *how* of this chapter.

I learned that God forgave me a long time ago for all the things I did before.

For all the fussing and cussing and being disgusted with life.

This man wanted to make me his wife.

He got on one knee and proposed to me.

Said some of the sweetest things a man ever said to me.

He loved me and I loved him. It's not the same as all the times before.

This time, I love me too.

I learned to love me.

I learned that I deserve love.

I learned that my past is just that... my **past**.

Trouble don't last always (shout out Rev Timothy Wright) and now I have better days (shout out Diane Reeves). So I pray...

Dear God,

Thank You for never giving up on me. Thank You for being the Supreme Being You are and seeing that I'm not a lost cause. Thank You for standing by me when I couldn't stand myself. Thank You for Your blessing and Your grace and Your mercy and Your favor. Thank You for my mama and, yes, even for my ... man with the last name...ok... my daddy. I forgive him just like You forgive me. Now I see that's all You wanted from me. For me to forgive and to love and to put You first. Thank You for building my character. That's what all those hard times were. You needed to know my character and what I would do in adversity. I tried to go out but instead I kept on pushing through. You always knew I would. You are my friend. You know my beginning and my end. You know because You made me. You gave me life, not mama. You saved me from the witch, not mama. You blessed my soul and sent me that angel who loves me and married me. You made me and 'I will give thanks unto thee; for I am fearfully and wonderfully made.' Psa 139:14 (ASV).

Amen

    That's how I managed to make it through.

That's how I managed to do anything positive from all that negative way I was living even though I was giving it my all and busting my butt.

You say luck?

No sweetie.

That's nothing but the grace of God right there.

Okay, okay. I'm finally ok.

This time I really *am* okay.

I'm good.

It's all good.

It really *is* all good now.

Hallelujah!

Don't have to get out of this place anymore.

What was that place?

The place I had to get out of was my own head,

that dread, that deadness inside,

where I would hide, and wither away, and give it away,

and take whatever they were giving out that day.

The place I had to get out of was the shame and the sadness and the regret

and the scrunched up face looking all ugly and twisted and frowned up hard.

The place I had to get out of was the gutter with the potty mouth

and all the shouting my soul was doing from the hurt from my dad.

The place I had to get out of was the low, low, way down low sadness and anger I had,

not anger towards others, but towards myself.

For letting it go this far.

For not telling, for not screaming, for not shouting, for not releasing

all the pain that I never should have been holding on to in the first place.

The place I had to get out of was the despair, the anguish,

the yearning for someone instead of for God.

The misplaced trust in people that only let me down every time

because I was trying to make them live up to expectations that had formed in my

head from fairytales and make believe stories I was read just before bed.

The place I had to get out of was my own way.

Sometimes you're in your own way.

      That's all I had to do. All I had to say was 'no' to the ones who wanted

to use me, abuse me, lose me, and toss me to the side when they were done.

All I had to say was 'go away' to the ones who wanted to take away my virtue,

my dignity, my soul, my happiness, my laughter,

make me grow old and bitter.

Make me a quitter.

Make me feel bitter and lower than low.

That's all I had to do..was say no.

So now I go and give my life to Christ, again.

Oh of course I did when I was little and I always knew He was there.

He was with me.

Sometimes I felt forsaken, but I knew He was still there.

I knew that He cared.

I knew He was watching even when I was doing dirt.

I always had faith and a connection.

      I went to join church when I was probably only five years old.

The Reverend *opened the doors of the church* and I went up.

My mama grabbed my wrist and asked if I knew what I was doing.

I promptly said a bold "Yes", but I didn't know the full extent of it.

I didn't know that I'm loved when I'm doing right but even when I'm doing wrong.

I'm loved no matter what.

Just like a mama loves their baby...or at least how a mama *should* love her baby....

no matter what.

I didn't know what all the Reverend *said* that day, but I knew what I *felt*.

I knew I needed to go to up there.

Not because other people were doing it.

Not because it was the right thing to do.

Not because someone said I'm supposed to.

But because I felt it in my heart.

I felt that call.

You may say "No way.

You couldn't possibly have known that young".

But I say nay to that.

I knew exactly where my heart was at (behind that preposition...naw, just kidding).

I knew beyond a shadow of a doubt what that was all about.
It was about love. I didn't understand most of the sermons each Sunday, but I liked going to church and listening anyway.
Some things stuck and some rolled off because the words were too big, but I knew how I felt.
I knew that something inside me pulled me to get up out of my seat, off of the pew.
I knew what I had to do.
I had to go up to the front.
Give myself and my life up.
I didn't know that was what it was called then.
After all, I was just a kid. I just knew what I felt.
I felt love.
I felt peace.
I felt safe.
I felt happy.
That day was a good day.
All the crazy that happened after that day made me forget a little.
I never really forgot, but I just didn't feel worthy.
Now I know I'm worthy.
Was always worthy.
No matter what others did to me or I did to myself.
No matter what craziness I invited into my life.
It all worked out and I knew that it would.
I knew that there must have been a plan for me even if it was one I couldn't see.

'As the heavens are higher than the earth, so are My ways higher than your ways, and My thoughts than your thoughts'. Isa 55:9 (NIV)

No, I couldn't see it.

I was short sighted.

I only saw the bad and not enough of the good.

I knew I should not be so jaded, but who could blame me?

I was tormented from so early on.

From so many things that went wrong. I made bad choices.

Listened to the voices in my head instead of the love in my heart.

Instead of the real friend who was on my side the whole time.

Rooting for me to cross the finish line into the light...

no...not the light they say you see when you're about to die.

The light of the truth.

The light of the promises.

The light of life

and happiness

and friends

and love

and laughter

and sunshine

and even rain.

Rain washes away the dust and rinses off the pollen,

carrying it to wherever it needs to go to make the next flowers grow.

That's the kind of light that makes you free.

Free from all the negativity.

The light that casts shadows away and makes for a better day.

The light that lifts your spirits when you're down and makes smiles out of frowns.

    I'm glad I found my light again. I'm glad I found myself a friend.

I'm glad I stopped all that sin. Ok, I'm not perfect. I'm a work in progress.

But now, in this light, this light that's shining directly on me like a spotlight,

it's like I'm on top of that table again shouting "I---!"

and rocking my hips from side to side.

It's like I'm singing my song and not shy at all.

It's like I've forgiven those fake, phony friends and all that craziness is so distant.

Not gone, but just a faint memory.

And this isn't the mind protecting me from something traumatic.

It's just my mind being set free.

Free of all of it.

'Free at last. Free at last. Thank God Almighty, I'm free at last.'

Shout out Rev. Dr. Martin Luther King, Jr.

Chapter 6: Why?

Why is all this so important? Why am I even sharing all this with you?

Is any of it even true? It's up to you. You believe what you want to.

Remember that car crash analogy?

I'm telling one version of the car crash. Is it really mine?

Is it live or is it Memorex? (old commercial shout out)

You believe what you want about it. All or none of it.

Why is that okay with me?

It doesn't matter if you believe me.

It doesn't matter if it's true or not.

All that matters is what you get out of it.

Can you relate to anything I had to say?

Can you identify with the broken, withered,

and damaged little flower in any way?

Have you had some of the same experiences?

Similar?

Exact?

Pieces missing or all intact?

Why do I want to tell you all of this?

Why?

I would be remiss if I didn't share something else with you.

Know this.

There is truth in every version of the car crash.

Every person has their own truth.

The sequence of events may be told differently.

Some of the facts stand out more than the others depending on who's telling their story.

There are three versions of the truth.

There's the truth of the definition of the words,

there's the truth of the intention of the person who spoke the words,

and there's the truth of the interpretation of the person who hears the words.

Living in three-part harmony like an old fashioned love song.

Shout out Three Dog Night.

Why does anyone tell a story? Because stories have a moral.

What's the moral of this story? Life happens.

You can either suffer through it or be blessed and learn from it.

You can either keep making the same mistakes over and over

and beating yourself up each time,

or you can find a lesson,

or even a blessing,

and not make the same mistake twice.

'Fool me once, shame on you. Fool me twice, shame on me'.

Shout out PFC Gomer Pile, USMC. Yes he's a TV character but it's still a good line.

I know I'm silly.

My husband says 'no matter what you do, always have fun'.

I agree. I laugh at myself a lot now.

There was a time when I didn't know why I was laughing all the time.

I was always smiling or laughing. No one ever really knew how sad and broken I was.

How did I hide it?

How did I fight the tears in public?

I guess I was always smiling because I refused to have my joy stolen.

But if you looked at my face, you may have seen the tracks of my tears.

Shout out Smokey Robinson and the Miracles.

Now don't get me wrong,

life with Mr Right is not all peaches and cream

and strawberry dreams

and rainbows and lollypops.

No, sometimes we got our set of troubles.

See, we both had a ready-made family. I have one and he has three.

So there was bound to be some struggles as we were trying to learn one another.

Learn our ways, our buttons not to push, our sensitivities, our subtle insecurities

...and those not so subtle.

Yes, I know we love one another, but there is probably sometimes gonna be a struggle.

That's life. That's to be expected.

But some things aren't what I predicted.

Sometimes things get to be a little hectic.

But for the most part, things are good.

I love him and he loves me.

A real love that I was searching for, for so long.

He's such a good man. God sent me someone to love after all.

      Life for me ain't been no crystal stair. Shout out Langston Hughes.

But I made it through. I found my way through all the craziness.

I reclaimed the love I used to have.

Reclaimed the love I had when I was with Amelia and Sasha

swinging and singing in the back yard.

Reclaimed the love I had when I was home

with Delia and LeShae and Ellis and Robert and Yolanda and mama...

and yes, even daddy.

No we don't talk but at least I've found forgiveness.

I found my joy.

I'm happy for the most part.

Of course things happen that you have to work through, but now I know what to do.

First I pray.

Then I try to listen and follow through.

Life is good.

It *really is* good.

I know I'm a blessed and highly favored. Shout out Clark Sisters.

      Why do I say all that I've said in each chapter?

It's to help the next person see their struggles through and do what they have to do.

You may follow a different path and do it a different way,

but at the end of the day, it's all the same.

Reclaim your light.

'Do not go gentle into that good night'. Shout out Dylan Thomas.

'Fight the good fight of faith; lay hold of the eternal life to which you were summoned' 1 Tim 6:12.

Make your presence known and don't cower to anyone or anything.

Stand tall.

Stand strong.

Be the best you and do what you want to do…within reason.

Don't do anything illegal or nothing…I'm just saying.

But know the sky is the limit and you can soar as high as you want and be safe.

Find your safe place.

Don't get out of any place because someone is taunting or something is haunting you.

Tell someone if you need to.

Talk to someone.

Don't keep it all inside and try to hide and swallow your pride and be dead inside.

Don't do what I did. Not even if you're a kid.

Someone will listen and someone will believe.

Just breathe and go forward.

Keep pushing forward. 'Keep on moving, don't stop, no'. Shout out Soul II Soul.

   Go back to those songs that you remember that give you inspiration.

like...

'Bright sunshiny day'—Johnny Nash, 'Let the sun shine in'—Aquarius,

'Joy to the world, all the boys and girls'—Three Dog Night,

'Jesus loves me, this I know, for the bible tells me so'—Anna B Warren.

Jesus loves you even if you've done wrong.

'While we were still sinners, Christ died for us'. Rom 5:8 (CEB).

'We are one'—Frankie Beverly and Maze. ...wait,

did I just put a Frankie Beverly song next to scripture?

Snickering...

We are all the same.

Less difference than we think.

We can help one another through the struggles

if we just tell someone what we're going through. And then there's...

'Yesterday'—Mary Mary. Oh this song, you gotta hear this song!

The words are so powerful. Check this out...

   'I had enough heartache and enough headache.

   I've had so many ups and downs.

   Don't know how much more I can take, mmmh.

   See I decided that I cried my last tears yesterday.

   Mmmh hmmm.

   Either I'm go'n trust You,

   or I may as well walk away.

   'Cause stressing don't make it better.

> Don't make it better no way.
>
> See I decided mmmh,
>
> that I cried my last tears yesterday.
>
> Yeah yesterday, oh yesterday,
>
> I decided to put my trust in You.
>
> Oh, oh, yesterday, yesterday,
>
> I realized that You would bring me through.
>
> There ain't nothing too hard for my God, no.
>
> Any problem that I have, He's greater, greater than them all.
>
> So I decided that I cried my last tear, yesterday'.

Those lyrics are so powerful! So don't cry anymore.

And don't ignore the power in you.

'You are of God, little children, and have overcome them:

because greater is He who is in you than he who is in the world'. 1 John 4:4

(WEB).

Little boy or little girl don't be ashamed

or sad

or wish you had done this or that.

It's okay, it's okay.

You *are* going to be okay.

Really.

There's so much more to tell. More about my childhood, the real friends I had,

being in the middle school band, the poems I would write,

the conversations I had with myself at night,

work and work friends,

all the travels over and about and back here again.

Tell you about my crazy friends.

There were a lot of good times despite some of the drama.

More to tell about my brothers and sisters and mama.

More to tell about Mr Right and our kids.

Good Lord, those kids!

They gave us a fit with some of the things they did.

That's a whole other story.

Maybe I'll tell you about all this in the next chapter. So keep a lookout.

To be continued...

www.ingramcontent.com/pod-product-compliance
Lightning Source LLC
Chambersburg PA
CBHW052113070526
44584CB00017B/2460